Quicksand/
Stargazing

Remi Recchia

Quicksand/Stargazing

Cooper Dillon

Quicksand/Stargazing
Copyright © 2021 by Remi Recchia
All rights reserved. First edition.

Cooper Dillon Books
San Diego, California
CooperDillon.com

Cover Design & Interior by Adam Deutsch
Author image by EricJ

ISBN-13: 978-1943899-14-2

Table of Contents

Head Space	1
Self-portrait as Ghost	2
Sleep Paralysis	3
Aubade	4
At the Stillwater, Oklahoma, Botanic Gardens	6
When the otter drowned at Binder Park Zoo,	7
When we don't invite your older brother to the wedding & your mother wants to know why,	8
Prosopagnosia Feels Like Looking Through a Tunnel and Landing in a Graveyard	9
When My Wife Cuts Her Hair & I Forget What to Say	10
Paris, Spring 2020	12
Pastoral #1	14
Waking Up from Top Surgery in a Sparse Airbnb Living Room	16
Vital Signs	17
A Trans Man's Guide to Using the Public Bathroom	18
Stain	21
Walking with My Lover to Bury Our Dead Fish	22
Dear Ex-boyfriend,	24

Eulogy	26
Ghazal for a Business Trip	28
Sunrise	29
Fratercula Cirrhata, or Boy Crossing	30
Reflections on a Punnett Square	33
The Sanderson Sisters Take Flight	34
Fire Eater, Premolar, Bone	35
Dressing as a Trans Man in the Early Morning	38
Cosmetology	39
Pastoral #6	41
The Ostriches Bathe in Tulsa, Oklahoma	43
Ghazal for the End of the World	45
Family Histories	47
Notes	58
Acknowledgments	59

For Roseanna: my beautiful wife, my life, the Capricorn of my arrival.

Head Space

After Tünde Darvay

My hands are sometimes
corduroy & I'm wondering

if I still fit inside your jeans,
inside your lightbulb pocket.

I can still see your breath, dank
river drivel & stale mint, pressing

syllables on my cheek & leaving
wet traces for days. Diogenes

feeds the animals—probably
their last meal—under harsh

kitchen fluorescence, knowing
these wolves will swallow

his last paycheck. They are bristle-
yellow & ghost teeth, thorned

parasite grip. What no one
tells a man is he will always

remember his first abuser,
house-key love turned to ash

inside a see-through vase. His
body an upside-down flower.

Self-portrait as Ghost

I don't miss the blood coating
inner thigh warmth: the first
of each month sneaking trickster
changeling through uterus & hips.

My wastebasket is lined with so
many costumes, underwear
worn & not worn, binders broken
& binders sewed. Ask a cis man

what's in his dresser. He doesn't know.
Ask a trans man what's in his. Watch
heavy feet smother worn-down carpet
leading to the closet. He'll open the door

slowly, stand back to let you
see. Watch him count needles,
vials, expired prescriptions
dating yearly checkups.

When the doctor asks me if I want
a pap smear because I've still *got
the parts*, she doesn't consider
the humiliation, the emasculating

shame exposing me to my wife.
When the drive-through worker
calls me *ma'am*, he doesn't apologize
when we pull up to the window.

Have you heard of phantom trauma?
The lick that's not quite pain, imagined
grief housed in bones, undetected?
Silas Weir Mitchell would pay to study

my lips, my skin, my spine. I have given
good money to shed my lips, my skin,
my spine. Still tiny tremors & earthquakes
touch my hips. Still I feel the seismic.

Sleep Paralysis

It starts slowly. I'm lying in bed, sober and still, feeling my wife breathe against my ear. Her breath is warm and a little sour, and my legs contour themselves to her form. The moon is nothing outside. I'm staring through the window slats. The other day I remembered something trivial about childhood, then I forgot it, then it said hello in a dream, and that might mean something. The pillow below my head is either too high or too flat. My feet are blistering furnaces. I have already turned over four times. And then: shoulders locking into place, body sinking into itself. I can't raise my arms or call her name. The moon won't do it for me. Other times my father—dead six years—asks me what I want to eat. I can't answer him, so I receive nothing. The moon won't do it for me. Or I'm napping in the office alone, and I see, with brilliant clarity, my colleague on a chair watching me. Her hair is bright, and I don't recognize the expression on her face. She says nothing. I say nothing.

I think of the countryside, the purple sleep-dots miraging themselves into one large man my sister couldn't see. I was afraid for so long and if I had to choose, I'd say that's when everything started: needing company, seeing signs, writing this life out of my mind. The paralysis always stops in the morning. My wife puts cinnamon in the coffee before work. I drive into the sun.

Aubade

Some days, after lovemaking in the unthinkably golden dawn, I stare at the crisscross train tracks on my chest under dark brown

bristled hairs. Raised lines thinning every day. Sighing just under flat pink nipples. I hear your heartbeat in my thumb. I taste your

pulse always. My chest is more expensive than yours, which makes it, in American terms, more beautiful. Did Christ

appraise his wounds for insurance? Did he print ICD-9 code 302.85 in careful butterfly hand? The holes in his sides

echoes of children acting out for attention. *Jimmy took my toy. Alice won't stop bruising me. My parents fight when they think I'm not*

listening. The Romans vied for love that only God could give them. Last year someone asked what He would think. That He

makes no mistakes. To that I'd say, no, He doesn't, but I was a small thing born in the small of the morning and maybe

that disrupted the natural progression of things. Maybe this life is the natural progression of things.

When we married in the dusty western heat—dancing to an orchestra of cicadas and horseflies and my dad's guitar, his

Gibson weeping for the end of an era—I felt the sweat baptize my skin in unreachable places.

You baptize my skin in unreachable places.

Our bedroom is humid and still. We both forget to clean but that's okay: large insects still wake us in the thrill of the morning.

My sponge kisses soft skin in the shower.
I bathe with the lights off—not because I don't want to see,

but because I've already memorized my body. My scars are not battle wounds, they're the map to the fight in the shadow of the

valley of death that I've already won.

At the Stillwater, Oklahoma, Botanic Gardens

Your aunt took us to the gardens in Missouri
two years before she died. The carp fish
orange in their private lake, pruned hedges
blinking like statues. I'm not afraid of death
but I think I'd miss you if you left
your hairbrush on the wood dresser without
new follicles, or your favorite cheese left
to spoil. A bird swallows

insects by the path. He is large and puffy,
unchanged by winter diet. He is just a decoy,
standing guard to alert other birds to predators.
His beak chatters in the breeze.

The coronavirus spreads its crown like a drunk
driver through the city, wrapping angel wings
around tree trunks and fence posts. The mayor
says *Keep your distance. Stop kissing in the moonlight. Stay away from your aunt's grave.*

But we visit when we can. We bring your aunt
candy wrappers and a Walmart discount
mourning plant. It was on clearance all week
hanging sadly in the corner. You named him
Fern and I fed a five into the self-checkout
slowly, watching for teeth or shredding.

When the otter drowned at Binder Park Zoo,

we did not go back for his funeral. Small, round, a thing of white
blubber and sleepy face—did he forget how to swim?

Did his handler decide, one day, that he'd been handled
enough, that he didn't need supervision each day? Local

television announced his death on the 7:00 news:
Today, our beloved Battle Creek otter, Mr. Sam, was found

drowned under his favorite rock. A brief silence on air.
We will miss Mr. Sam greatly. The otter's death a certain

kind of escape. Maybe otters are never as happy
as they seem. Maybe they tire from attention, from holding

hands with their spouses as they bathe in salty waves
for our sinister, voyeuristic pleasure. Maybe the otter divorce

record is higher than humans': floppy black hands stained
with seaweed ink from signing their names here, here,

and here, with X'd initials here, here, and here. What
does it take to kill a marriage? An affair, a missing

child, a decades-long misunderstanding. We shiver in front
of the television. We'd seen that otter on our first date

years ago, holding the lemonade and veggie burgers
I'd bought for us at the overpriced Sea World Adventure

kiosk. We talked about small children, family wills, where
we wanted to place our DNR tattoos—everything

we would never need to know. Now we're in the living
room, the otter's bloated corpse weighing on our senses,

still tasting a burned curry dinner, wondering not *how*
but *why it took him so long to do it.*

When we don't invite your older brother to the wedding & your mother wants to know why,

we're not quite sure what to say. How to say
her son is not the man she thinks he is, to say
her son hates her youngest daughter, to say
yes, I suppose I'm replacing him.

You send your brother a letter. I send him a letter.
His letter-opener falls behind the stove, or the blade
dulls, or the letter gets lost in the mail, or he burns
the letter like a scarlet fever.

I feel an old bruise on my abdomen. I find
old paperwork, dig a grave in the backyard.
I drown my dead name, old driver license,
undergrad college degree in cow manure.

I get lost on the Internet for hours. Ohio
tells me we shouldn't bother moving closer to my
parents. The state of Michigan tells me not to start
a family. You tell me you don't sleep when I'm gone.

We keep a careful spreadsheet of bylaws, court
cases, political stances of house representatives.
You say I'm not the problem, & maybe
that's true, & maybe I need your dad to love me.

We send your mother an extra Christmas gift
wrapped like a cobbler gluing shoes, silent work
under dim light. You are asleep & snow is tapping
the window, a quiet wind melting through the door.

Prosopagnosia Feels Like Looking Through a Tunnel and Landing in a Graveyard

I read recently that face-blindness
can be caused by trauma,
but I don't know which trauma
caused what or why sometimes
I have scars and sometimes I don't.
I don't know how old I am
when I know this. I'm seven years old
and we're at the zoo, or I'm twelve
years old at the aquarium. I'm smart
but not face-smart. There are too
many people in the crowd. The crowd
is one watercolor person, all faces blending
together into something I can't recognize.
My mother is a stranger. I have hugged
the wrong stranger. I hug another stranger.
She's not right, either. I go up to each
person in the room, every time pressing
close to the wrong person. My mind is
three steps forward or three steps
back—I can't see anything in order.
I go to the bathroom and have a staring
contest with the mirror. It is only me
and this strange boy in the mirror.
I do not recognize my face but I recognize
my tongue, salty and wet and small.

When My Wife Cuts Her Hair & I Forget What to Say

I sometimes forget to smile at my friends
& lovers. I assume they're already in my head

space, that they know what I'm thinking.
I try to make up for it at the grocery store,

let others cut me in line or grab the last
bargain just in case I know them. My

doctor holds up signs of faces: happy,
sad, neutral. That feeling you get when

you find the last zucchini in the barrel.
I practice emoting on my face. Quick!

How to look when your friend cremates
his family dog?

How to smile when your partner is promoted
at work?

My heart beats red for others, yet my lips
remain pressed and neutral. I'm a J. C. Penney

mannequin: tall, fake, & pointless—
we all know how our clothes will fit before

we try them on: uncomfortably. After 10
years of marriage, I came home to a pixie-cut

stranger in my bedroom. The black lace
clung to her in all the right places, perfect

skin illuminated by vanilla candles, but still
I almost called the cops because I knew

my wife had long hair. My darling, she laughed,
it's just me. This is what forgetting how to smile

feels like. I miss other people's faces &
therefore miss my own. Someone please tell me

what I look like in the mirror. The steam
reflects my wanting.

Paris, Spring 2020

My father is in Paris. He's old, short-sighted, has papery skin & a bad foot. He's begging to be another bird on the Paris streets across the Atlantic— he won't come home, doesn't believe in the virus —but I fill the birdfeeder tray in case he wants to leave the burial nest. My palms sweated through the *New York Times*, crinkled in my fist when I knew of the 25,000+ French deaths, forgot to pray as the widowmaker's crowned spikes took Paris.

I don't remember my first steps, but I know they were late because my dad wouldn't stop holding me. I stood on my legs like a tiny giraffe & fell over in the Luxembourg Gardens & cried needlessly, probably. I was always crying, he always soothing, catching baby spittle on his shoulder while humming Elvis songs or watching TV. I'm not crying now, just worrying my wife to annoyance, & dinner plates slip right out of my hands onto the waxy kitchen floor. We've gone through so many dishes we shouldn't even eat anymore, just crouch in front of the TV & tally the death count. Let's play a drinking game: one shot for every science denier. One shot for each country that goes on lockdown. Twelve for every parent who might already be gasping through a ventilator. I wonder if my father's lungs are weak from smoking.

Paris, my dad says, is the place for writers. He keeps a running list of American expatriates: James Baldwin, F. Scott Fitzgerald, Ernest Hemingway. He wants to live there, too, to leave his Midwestern life behind. I don't tell him that Paris smells like piss, that I have seen more drunken bar fights there than anywhere else, that I can't walk without tripping over a dozen pigeons. So I listen to him on the phone saying he doesn't need to come home, saying the coronavirus will not, in fact, kill him. What I hear is that I should prepare for orphanhood. I get my act together & write a will for my future children. I unplug the phone when we hang up, stop sending postcards in the mail.

13

Pastoral #1

The cows are misting
silent, burrowed in white
softness & sky-down.

I'm driving & you are
golden, counting seconds
against the digital

clock of our old car
(three accidents later,
motor still warm, dash

dented with a yellow
bruise). Do you ever
wish we weren't here?

We are fixtures of other-
ness, one brown cow
among the spotted herd.

Rural eyes & cardinal
sins, they are our gate-
keepers, as if we need

one reason to leave.
I want to say I'm used
to this turning, these fists

hovering over my small
face. I'm used to this
orange scrutiny. But you

are not & I don't want
you to know we're alone,
so let me be your star.

We'll paint the sky-canvas
splotchy cow colors
accented with sober love.

Keep me in the dark. Hold
dirty towels, always, stark
neon against the pasture.

Waking Up from Top Surgery in a Sparse Airbnb Living Room

My breasts are gone.
Orange lights seep through the blinds,
caressing my wife's face
as she worries the kitchen clean.

The hardwood floor
reflects my new watch, large
face swallowing wrist:
a reminder that I am a man.

My body now a map instead of a globe,
rivered with lines and incisions.
Heavy bandages and compression
protect my newfound flatness.

I am heavy and still with Percocet.
My wife keeps a medication chart
at her bedside; she kneels and washes
my feet with a borrowed cloth.

If I stood, I know I would rise
like a Lazarus in the heat of certainty.

Vital Signs

I talk to my mother-in-law more
than my own mother, & maybe
that's because we're friends, or maybe
because I think I might not know
how to die without my wife nearby.

I bring my mother-in-law tea at the
nursing home. The tea is weak; I
complain for her because she's too
polite to protest. I lift the porcelain
to her lips on Sundays after church.

My wife is busy. I have picked out
a shared burial plot for our parents:
small churchyard cemetery & tree-root.
I've watched both mothers, both fathers
sign D.N.R. on hospital paperwork.

I take my mother-in-law out to vote
in a wheelchair. She is a tiny, trembling
grace, working out the knots in the system.
We read each other bedtime stories
in the morning because she falls asleep

too early, breath loud & sour, while I
wait for room service & a put-upon
hospice worker. The worker takes my
mother-in-law's pulse, sometimes gives
it back.

A Trans Man's Guide to Using the Public Bathroom

Lick the sweat from your wrist
quietly. The sound of porcelain
flush startles you, but your feet
do not jump.

*

Other men come in like
bulls. They do not knock.
Keep the stall door
locked and swaddled.

*

No talking, no eye-contact
rubber meeting truth. No
pupils dilate nor hardness
rise.

*

The mirror is dirty. You
are dirty. The men, staring
bullets into their reflections
over the water head, have
occupied the sink. You may
not wash your hands.

*

Sometimes there are no locks.

*

It is better to piss your pants
than to dawdle.

Better to use less toilet paper
than rattle the roll.

*

The crack in the stall door
begs invitation. Decline it.

*

Do not check your packer,
binder in the mirror. At best,
it will lie to you, and you can't
afford to look small.

*

Walk in chest forward—swagger—
but eyes down. You may hold the door
open for the next man, but briefly.
One second is sufficient.

*

Dead fly-wings and earwax
eat themselves slowly in the pit
of your stomach. Wasps mate
in your eyeballs where you let
yourself get too thin.

*

Remember not to pop your hip
or rest your arm on air. This is
not the radio; you are not a star.

*

Tell your wife where you are,
how long you'll be. Take your
phone with you. You never know
when a man will take it upon
himself to show everyone what
real men are and what they are not
and why risk something so delicate,
so unsure.

Stain

A splinter kissed my ring
finger today, sharp tooth

rooting into flesh. I feel its dull
head all day. Spear positioning

itself like a trout. I remember
my old address, the mulberry

tree outside my house standing
like a watchman. Its branches

tall, thick. Purple in summer.
I remember what invasion

tastes like. I feel his hands
again, rubbing circles on my dry.

Mouth cracked open. Roommates
away that morning. The splinter

loves me. The splinter
wants to stay.

Walking with My Lover to Bury Our Dead Fish

Slow-breathed and boot-clad, we
walk to the lake with our dead Betta
fish in hand. You placed her tail-
down in a children's beach
pail. It's midnight and we are not
supposed to be out, but at least
here the reeds will mourn for us, make
space for our empty teeth. The stars
swarm like golden mosquitoes. I can taste
fresh humming in my throat. My feet
slip when we meet the dock. We hold the pail
together. The pail is still. Our pale
hands are still. Had our mouths been
moving, dead language would have wrinkled
currents deep within the lake. You wrinkle
currents deep within me. When I proposed
last year, I felt your *yes* settle
inside my chest. I adore you through bed-
sheets, through dinner, through trinkets
snatched like a magpie, so many tokens
cluttering your dresser. We swaddle each
other in bubble wrap every morning. No
bruises here, we say. Pass the bubble
wrap. Can a fish be tucked
safe in bubble wrap? I suppose we didn't try
hard enough, and now we'll never know, but my
darling, all I want now is to propose
over and over and over again, read
yesyesyes on your lips, scoop
you back home. I want to live in your soft
thighs. You let me enter each night; my body
never wants to leave, but first we have to let
go the thing we could have raised
together. We turn the plastic bucket
upside down, fish so small she doesn't even
splash. I see one pink fin poke through coarse
gravel. And then the moon wakes up blazing

silver, and the lake is illuminated—
your eyes reflect everything that has ever
been perfect, and it's almost like we never
killed anything at all.

Dear Ex-boyfriend,

let me be the first to tell you being your first was not a victory
it was a nettlesome papercut & a waste of condom

I don't miss you like I should or maybe like I could
I rarely think of you these days but I thank you
for giving me your favorite Radiohead album

your music has a much better home now
by which I mean my car & not your embarrassment

when we were in college you named your fish Ophelia
& no one bothered to tell you how fucked up
that was

sometimes I remember your shrill laugh & cold, wet
mouth & how for a long time I thought I hated kissing,
but now I'm grateful for the reminder that most boys
are just not good kissers

I was not a boy when we were together—what did that make us?

Old Navy sells a hoodie just like yours: gray
& striped & clearance'd for seven dollars
I purchased the damn thing & now I wonder if we're more
alike than I'd like

your dick is not the punchline but if it were I'd say
I found its crookedness strange, its skin unnerving
sleeping with you was like looking at a faceless snake
with too many tails

Steve, you have ruined engineers for me forever, &
I'm not sorry because your name is fucking Steve

I think if we'd met now we'd get along
just two nerdy guys talking about nothing

remember when we went to Sonic & we ordered
milkshakes? I wanted the small, but you insisted
child-sized for me, said that was large enough

now I am a boy with my own girl—what does that make me?

I want so badly to redeem you in this poem
some men are not worth the time
you are not especially worthy of anything
though I will say thank you for the scarf
when I was cold
thank you for the pregnancy scare
in that it was just a scare

I don't think you'd be a bad father but I know
we'd have reset the world's divorce record

I never liked your Pomeranians, little
furry rats poised, spoiled, on the couch

I won't give you credit for my personal growth,
though, selfishly, I might take credit for yours
isn't that what we do?
we fuck, we love, we dance with other humans
hoping to someday wake up as a star

Eulogy

> *Frost and freeze conditions will kill crops, other sensitive vegetation, and possibly damage unprotected outdoor plumbing. Take steps now to protect tender plants from the cold. To prevent freezing and other possible bursting of outdoor water pipes, water pipes should be wrapped, drained, or allowed to drip slowly.*
>
> —*Stillwater, Oklahoma, Weather Forecast*

Under deer's eyes and a gray sky, I am driving
you to the airport. The orange Oklahoma sunrise
sleeps, still. Everything is asleep except us.

Your energy is a nervous battery: your eyelashes
witness the time, the radio. Your boarding pass
collects sweat under pale fingers. I've never been to a funeral:

dark masses of ceremony and ash. I don't know
what a dead body smells like. What goes into
a eulogy? Something about the senses, the smell

skin sings after lovemaking, or what a body
count means to us. Something about surrender
or Christ or beauty. There is nothing beautiful

about death. I rap my knuckles on the steering
wheel, wonder what to say. I'm sorry your mother
is dead. I'm sorry your father is dead. I'm sorry

I couldn't take that call for you. The car almost
refused to start last night after work. I took it
for a test drive, wanted to feel moonbeams

kiss my bare chest. The bristled black hairs around my collar-
bone hid themselves from the stars. My teeth
ached as I sat down in the grass. I wanted to eulogize

your parents, both of them, and their marriage,
considered forging your signature beneath a poem
snuck deep inside your pocket. But I didn't

write them last night, and I didn't write them
this morning, and I still don't know what to say,
the car's headlights harsh and golden and brave.

Ghazal for a Business Trip

The flight attendant is offering me drinks & oysters
I can't afford. Can she see my mind is elsewhere?

I showed up to the airport hungover, eyes
bloodshot, every pulse of me wanting to be elsewhere.

You called me the night before, but I couldn't reach
the phone. We don't know when I'm getting elsewhere.

My briefcase reeks of vomit. The cab driver agrees—
why couldn't he have picked up a pretty girl, driven elsewhere?

I went out & started tab after tab, rekindling
old friendships after living elsewhere.

The pilot's voice is loud on the intercom, directing
storm clouds & bird migrations elsewhere.

We both thought I could handle this trip.
I'm coming home after floating elsewhere.

But my pupils—dark, swollen—my forehead—
flushed with night sweat & booze bought elsewhere—

they tell me to stay away from the plane propeller, to not
take this life with a rope or blade elsewhere.

My pupils say, this shame won't pass, but you
don't have to speak, Remi, don't have to go elsewhere.

Sunrise

My father told me once that after gas stations
dry up, nothing can grow in their place.

Something about pipes & gasoline, ethanol
carcass splayed open like a dead animal. Imagine:

electric rubber cords pulsing in heat
across America. My shoes are wet with cooled

methanol, toes rubbing together like pigs
thrusting forward for slop. My heels are burning

sore redness through the soles. This paycheck
might die on its way to the bank in rural, cornfed

Ohio. The weeds look gray this August: ghost-
men standing still. Eat one flower petal & stay

underground forever. Letters can only flicker
neon for so long. The day can run out of light.

Fratercula Cirrhata, or Boy Crossing

> *A significant decline in numbers of puffins on the Shetland Islands is worrying scientists.*

I buried my Russian Nesting Doll
in the dirt, red paint blooming
up like a worm carcass. Color
dissolves like a succulent.

My sister—with scissors & glue
dripping funeral march—went looking
under gray sky & cough syrup
clouds. Came back empty-handed.

Father came home from work
one-booted & barren, kissed
Mother hello with tang & bleary
eyes, no paycheck.

*

Added to the grave at night: one
Minnie Mouse wristwatch, two
pink barrettes. I slept outside &
kept watch with the dark.

I am my sister's keeper, she
Mother's helper. That meat
won't cook itself, & Father
will not wait.

*

My mouth can carry several
teeth at one time. My mouth
can carry several lies at one
time.

After the burial: sleepless
interludes until I became ghost-
spider & vein-ridden, flattened
to the floor like old taxidermy.

*

I store fish inside a goose-
feathered pillowcase, tucked
safely behind the stairs. I
kiss them before dinner.

*

My snout aches.

*

My Father's mouth is a rudder,
my sister's mouth is a runner—
two always crashing, clashing
in the kitchen—show

me a lullaby & he'll beat you
to sleep, eyes closed, fists
half-carved with sunken
moon, sterile, clawed.

Mother wasn't home so we ate
her dinner. Mother wasn't home
so we took her bed. We stole
her jewelry box. We wore

her jewels while Father said
nothing, while he knocked
stale worries like ringworms
from my sister's teeth.

*

I left my sister at home surrounded
by cheap puzzle teeth & decayed
yarn—no heat forthcoming—I
packed my bags,

stole the car, ran a red light, thought
about going home twelve times &
just drove faster. I did not wait for
hitchhikers.

*

I dreamed I sprouted wings
last night. It was at the grocery
store, grand crescendo of freak
among watermelons & cherries.

A mother covered her child's
eye with a microscope, the floor
melted into kaleidoscope coupons
of gray, blue, green, everything

puffin imaginable, & I was big,
puffy, swollen as with the feathers
of Christ himself, Christ on the cross,
on the island.

Reflections on a Punnett Square

There must be something genetic about breaking
boundaries. How to slide off someone's underwear
in the dark. I wonder how it feels to jimmy

locked doors on top of tree houses &
ash.

Owl, in French, is *chouette*, presumably for the sound
dripping from its beak before dawn. Something is always
dripping from my beak before dawn.

My fingernails are sharp in the sunlight, shredded
aftertaste of force & want.

How true does something have to feel to matter?

Once I prayed so hard I turned into the sun.
That's not true, an owl.
That's not true, a mouse.
None of this is true.

Most days my cheeks are a cavern. If I see
you in a dream, I'm sorry.

I will forgive you if you pretend not to see me. I'll lock
your car for you while you walk into someone else's night.

The Sanderson Sisters Take Flight

It's said that Cuckoos will lay eggs in other birds' nests,
sing a crooked lullaby, & then—*now! you're mine*—or
maybe that's just from *Hocus Pocus*. A cowbird can lay

220 eggs in other species' nests, pushing out the OG
one feather at a time, but I lose 100 things a year & nobody
has even noticed. My talons seize up each time I meet

an infant's eye in his stroller or a proud toddler wearing
a ridiculously pink dress. I want to scoop them up, bring
them home & say honey, look what I found.

But I'm not Sarah Sanderson, I can't steal children, & I
haven't got a beak from which to sing, so instead I'll pace
& pace, beat down the living room rug, & pretend

I don't want another face in the mirror. My body is soft,
useless—it can't tango with my wife's eggs, so instead
I take her to a dance. We move my pathetic & her

yearning to an outdated Bette Middler tune, gazing
up at the disco ball overhead. I pretend the ball
hatches right then & there on the dance floor.

Everyone would be draped in sequins & feather
boas. Everyone would stop dancing. We would all
be silent & sober & still.

Fire Eater, Premolar, Bone

It's eight a.m. and the dentist has her hands in my mouth,
probing for something I don't understand. My tongue
fights against the pressure. I don't know anything
about teeth—not my own, not my lover's—but the dental
hygienist cradles my head, warms my chattering.

*

I was twelve when I had my first extraction: eight
stalactites tucked tight in a crooked cave. My gums
overcompensated for my smile.

*

Sometimes when we kiss, I feel your teeth
clink against mine: the quietest champagne
toast. We are not embarrassed anymore when this happens.

I am not embarrassed by most things.

*

My mouth is small, but that doesn't mean
no one has asked to be inside it.

*

A fire eater does not actually eat fire, nor
does he breathe it. It's a trick of blinding
light and gullibility and kerosene. All dragons
are dead.

*

A recurring dream: I am small. My teeth
won't stop growing. I open my mouth wider and wider,
choking on my newfound sabers, unable to regain
control. My mouth is a remote-control toy, and I
have lost the remote, or someone else has taken
it, or I do not know where the remote is.

*

Two boys bloodied my lip at age six.
This is not particularly surprising, though
I do wish it had only happened once.

*

I am not a fire eater and neither are you.
I have never swallowed a fire eater.

We go to the fire eater's show to feel something, wait
all day in line for even just the possibility of one
overpriced ticket. I won't throw my stub away
when it's over.

*

Another time, another place, a dentist
shames me into flossing. Your gums are angry,
she insists. They are inflamed. You just gotta suck
it up. She tells me her boyfriend is a princess.
He doesn't hunt or fish like her father.

*

I bought you a million gold castles in my mind
the first time we slept together. While I was inside
you, I kept thinking, your mouth is a home
I want to live in. Lips, please let me worship you.
I want to take communion under your tongue.

*

When I was young, I loved a girl with a tongue
piercing. She would roll it back and forth, a secret
game, a flirtation for the two of us. Now I am old
and I do not love her but that's okay because my gums
survived unscathed.

*

The roof of my mouth is permanently scarred.

I do not know if this is true.

*

A fire eater eats fire only in the eye of the public.
After work, the fire eater is sad or lonely, or he celebrates
his latest victory, the deceiving of small children, or he
thinks nothing of it. He buys a bag of grapes, picks
up a loaf of bread. He weighs a rotisserie
chicken in his wax-licked palm.

*

My cupboards are bare like teeth newly sprung
from metal braces: shiny, organized. Not a crumb
in sight.

*

I check my teeth in the mirror before our first
date. I stand in my best jacket. I am a showman like
the fire eater, but I won't make you pay to see
me up close.

Dressing as a Trans Man in the Early Morning

She makes sure my binder
is nice & tight against
swollen tumors leeching skin.
The packer is beige & bulging,
safely tucked in jeans too long
for my stature, straining to meet
strawberry standards of mass-
produced men & hormone-growth.
She eases the dark red pricks
from my needle-worn, pincushioned
body, my beautiful wife, my life,
the Capricorn of my arrival.
She peels Band-Aids like
yellow fruit from Eden.

Cosmetology

Sometimes in the morning I watch you in the mirror, memorize the shapes you make in the sink. I know which smile means something is funny, which laugh means you'll tell me later. I look for your father's nose, or maybe

his forehead, or his anything at all on your face because I wonder what our son would look like, a little bit of boy mixed in your complexion. But I only see your mother: soft cheeks blossoming pink against birch bark,

large eyes filling silences. I pick up the earring-backs adorning the counter & vacuum up fake nails from the stained living room carpet. Bobby pin casualties follow you to work, to school, to the store; the grackles and robins

know to come to our house in nest-building season. They cradle bobby pins tenderly in elegant black beaks & clever talons, the pins wrapped with whispers of golden hair. They need them to shelter brittle eggs, fragile tomorrows.

I add bobby pins to the shopping list for Walmart, & we place them carefully in the cart next to the eggs in a makeshift burrow. Later I brush an eyelash off your cheek in bed. You tell me to make a wish but I cheat,

I make one hundred & don't tell you what I wished for. We turn off the light before the wishing is over so I don't know if the eyelash falls to the floor, don't know if my wishes will hatch in the morning.

Pastoral #6

We're lying next to each other on Sunday morning, sleep-
flowers pressed in your eyes, five o'clock shadow on my jaw.
The Venetian blinds are half-drawn: fossil of wine & no
filter. *The slats can be rotated such that they overlap with one
side facing inward & then in the opposite direction such*

they overlap with the other side facing inward.
An old anniversary balloon wilts in the corner, & I'm reminded
of last October when the clerk ID'd me at the gas station,
said I'm too young to be married. What he didn't know is I
have already built a house, a home, a life.

My palms sweat your absence on business trips. They butterfly
your thigh at church. We administer our own communion.
*Between those extremes, various degrees of separation may be
effected between the slats by varying the rotation.* I haven't been
on a first date in so long, but darling, I've always known you.

There are also lift cords passing through slots in each slat—
& also the sun—there are also empty bottles on the counter—&
also the red-stained rug. *When these cords are pulled, the bottom
of the blind moves upward, causing the lowest slats to press
the underside of the next highest slat as the blind is raised.*

It took Christ four days to un-sleep Lazarus. We'll weather
last night out together for hours, your legs curled into mine
on a discount mattress & frayed blanket. A blue jay teaches
his children to fly outside the window. *A modern variation
of the lift cords combines them with rotational cords in slots*

on the two edges of each slat. The baby birds plummet to the ground
one after the other. Their father flies across the yard like a
machine. We model our behavior so children can grow
into their parents. *This avoids the slots otherwise required to allow
a slat to rotate despite a lift cord passing through it, thus decreasing*

the amount of light passing through a closed blind. Let the sun rise without us. Let's miss business hours. Let's fill our bellies on bread, on eggs, on cheese. You'll put cinnamon in my coffee. I'll drive you to work. There's only so much time to burn those feathers.

The Ostriches Bathe in Tulsa, Oklahoma

It's ninety-eight degrees out and we're walking,
foolishly, at the zoo. My arms are bare, already
sticky and burning. The back of my neck is wet.
I want a sexy way to tell you I just need to go
home and rest. The brim of your hat is broad.

When we moved to Oklahoma, you told me your hair
got big. At first it was funny: some frizzes
here and there, maybe some morning static. But then

we stayed longer and longer, and now we're still here,
and we buy expensive shampoo because your hair
demands more time, more attention. I won't demand
these things from you because your body needs it
more, but my darling, I can't wait to take you home.

You ask for a landline every day. That's not true.
I ask for a landline every day. I miss the way a cord
feels, coiled around the wrist or elbow. When I was young
I would watch my mother talk on the phone while she
did the dishes, the way her shoulder propped perfectly
the mouthpiece against her jaw. The plates never

broke. Bubbles made everything beautiful.
We're passing the prairie dogs now. One animal
digs alone, planting his face in the ground and wailing
his everything into the dirt. He's building a home
in the middle of nowhere.

The sun sinks through his coat. The air is quiet.
Anything that should be making noise
sleeps now. They'll eat later. I'm still not sure
how to feed us. Where do you buy food with no money?

Your parents think I've got a plan, but I don't, and we
are hungry, and we are young. Black asphalt
absorbs our footprints—a clean break from voyeur to nothing.

I think I'd like to be a fossil one day, have a scientist
break through my crust, my grief housed in bones.

I want her to peel through my remains and use me
for science. And before I can say your name and ask you
to take up chemistry, we make a wrong turn and approach huge
birds with shaggy brown-feathered shoulder blades. One ostrich
stares at us, unblinking. But the sun goes behind
us for one glorious second, and I see his friends,

also enormous and feathered with naked legs, eyes
like scales on a sunken ship, and they dance
in the unfathomable shade. A zookeeper stands above
and sprays their backs with a thick hose, and I see

everything I have ever wanted to see, both of us drenched
in sweat but stuck in place mere feet from the entrance, four
deadly birds rolling in pleasure, and then you're laughing
and I'm laughing and I almost run into the enclosure, into the
    rain.

Ghazal for the End of the World

Let's drink black coffee after our friends have stopped watching
    for the sun.
We'll stay up and gaze out the window, wait for the sun.

The pool is empty, our living room pillows scattered
like many feathered carcasses that bake in the sun.

Your brain went quiet for two weeks this month and it finally
came back, stopped its progression, fake, to stop the sun.

Is the moon an angel? Is the front porch my guardian?
I remember how birds used to mate on the stoop in the sun.

When I was a child, I couldn't stand the outside air.
Too bright, too loud, people and crowds, late in a million suns.

My wife's belly is still not round, and we can't fix it,
but still we buy baby clothes and wait for a son.

Our fathers are old, our mothers are young. Who
will COVID strike first with its lake fires of sun?

The night won't fade until it's called. We shudder
in the cold. I count my teeth and paint them for the sun.

I want to be your love song. Please hear me in the shower,
in the hall. My voice is too guttural. You may rate it against the
    sun.

My own reflection dazzles me: slight build of tremoring
white with blue eyes. I kneel before the traits of my father's son.

Once I stopped the car too soon. We flew, suspended, over
highway lanes and motorbikes. I stomped the brakes under the
    sun.

My father would squint for the camera only reluctantly.
I don't think he liked his face, a waste, under the sun.

It won't rise today, Remi, you've fallen for a cruel trick—
not of the light, but of the dawn, the fated invisible sun.

Family Histories

My grandmother is maybe from Pennsylvania
I don't know if Marcus was raped
So many men leaving, leaving, walking

upside down in that house of mirrors
Shards everywhere
Shards in the sink

Shards in the sink before you can blink

        Have you ever wondered why there are so many angels in the ocean?

Sometimes I've been alive for so long I can't STAND

                      this noise
                      your joy
                      won't employ
                      my emptiness

Never have I ever washed my hands
Never have I ever drunk a moat

Never have I ever bungee-jumped
off a cliff with the motor still running

It's hard to piece together family history when there are pieces
lost inside me, O Great Narrator—and now I see I address
myself—inside you is where I want to be but I don't fit yet
I am not large like the buttons on your raincoat

                        Star-crossed lovers are only star-crossed
                                                    at night.

                                   Traffic laws are meant
                                              to be broken.

I've never seen the point of a peaceful protest
If a man is grabbing you spear him straight to the dick
I wouldn't think twice about castrating my neighbor
He's so nosy and old and there

patty cake patty cake baker's bread * my mother told me to pick the very best one and you * listen to the
doorbell in the dead of everything * if a zombie's out there won't you let him in * we all ding-dong-
ditched at ten * but some of us stayed dead forever

Once in a car I googled signs of sociopathy
So worried I was that his night vision had rubbed off on me
I told a friend and laughed first to spare him
So many mechanical feelings in the sink

My lover and I like to walk in the graveyard
I'm sure it's sacrilegious—we're not paying tribute, just playing dead

One possum two possum three possum four. What do you smell like in the dark?

I dream about boarding school, the nuns ruling down my neck, or maybe a priest

Tell me: would you rather: hyperventilate forever OR
                             only walk in slow-motion?

Tell me: would you rather: forget your mother OR
                             forgive your father?

Tell me: would you rather: grow the same mustache forever OR
                             be a virgin each Tuesday?

I hate your smile
I hate your lips
I hate your grackle murmurings
I don't know who I am speaking to

        roses are red / violets are blue / I am not dead / how about you

Waking fills me with such ANXIETY
GOD can you IMAGINE getting up AGAIN
If I have to walk to the store today I might KILL MYSELF

At the grocery store, now, smoothing the skin of an onion
The bulb is precious and soft in my hands
My thumbs are rough from some weird sex act
I put the onion in my mouth, suck on its crinkled dryness

                              Is the beer still hair of the dog
                                    if you are cold when you
                                              swallow?

                              I sit at my desk in the morning
                                    and grieve the sun-
                                              light.

Moonbeams flickering through the window past my skull
I'm trying to remember my family's history
My father told it to me once in a not-moving car
I was young but old enough to pay attention

I was seven when I had my first drink, watered down and sweet
My mind lit up thirteen years later at a party
Now life is always a party and I am the carousel

Let me be: your:

        drug
        helicopter
        anchor
        party bus
        rehab clinic
        vessel to insert your dick
        dick inside your vessel

This poem isn't about me but I am convenient
This poem is about my family and the fucked-up secrets
we don't tell in the dark

Please buy me a Sharpie and tell me your worst nightmares
I want to draw those monsters and hold them up at a parade
Drag queens will throw glitter and coverup on my poster board
I might be your poster boy for Young or Lost or Addict

                                        If I sit at the bus stop
                                              will you wait
                                                    with me?

                                        Please don't make me
                                        spell it out for you.

My therapist wants to know about my hyperfocus
My intelligence, wants, needs, traumas, undiagnosed histories
I want to tell her stories about my concussions and vomit
My god have you ever seen so much blood

bent over the bathroom sink
                remembering something
                              remembering shards
                                          if I bend over be gentle when you fuck me

Jesus didn't forsake Judas but Judas hanged himself anyway
Sometimes it's like that in life if you can call this living anyway
I shoplift at Walmart even when I can afford nice clothes
Sometimes it's like that in life if you can call this living anyway

If you can call this life / please god can you take my life

If he raped me again I might know
how to handle it this time.

So rape me, I'm ready.
I can handle it.

These are the things I think about in the shower * april showers bring may flowers * may flowers bring pilgrims * and then there was a mass genocide * yes we're still recovering * no this will never be over

I don't know why I'm in therapy if I can just take pills forever
Doctor, please prescribe me some sleep for I am weak

Have you ever wondered why there are so many angels in the ocean?

Little Red Riding Hood is a LIE.
There is no way that girl was so brave
In real life she would have been dead: long before:

meeting the woodsman
straying from the path
holding her basket

I hold my basket like a casket
Please don't ask me to stay

I burn my underwear at night when I'm bored
Breathe in the fumes and cotton just to stay awake
I don't sleep for weeks because all I see is shards
Shards in the sink are like sharks on the beach:
appropriate but still startling

I am appropriate always but still startling
Something about me surprises people
Maybe if I knew what it was I could be better

One diagnosis that never goes away is talking too much

If this is talking too much / please god can you take my tongue

                                              What are fireflies
                                                in the sunlight?

If speeding is a crime then lock me up now
I don't think I'll ever take my foot off the gas
Take me in the ass or don't take me at all
If only my words would last or last or LAST

LAST night I dreamed I was a FATHER
I had small children and they were loved
I fed them ice cream every day until they bloated
They became sugar-balloons and drifted away

I like to pop my birthday balloons with a boxcutter
It is better than popping so many other things
When I was a child I had a dog and I loved him
Some things do not bear repeating

                                      If the match wants to be set on fire
                                    who will have the nerve to reach
                                                for the kerosene?

                       Burn me / churn me / say you won't turn me

I'm not away I'm just sleeping but I'm not home for you
Please take my silence as a sign: yes: it is personal
Maybe I hyperfocus but only when I see beauty
And beautiful things have a habit of passing me by

The insects built anthills outside my kitchen window
I bow to them every morning as I eat my toast
I think about taking the toaster to the bath with me
Instead I sit and drink coffee and call my dad on the phone

Have you ever wondered why there are so many angels in the ocean?

The angels bear repeating because of course they are beautiful
I wake up every morning wishing I had scales or a dorsal fin
Can you imagine: those colors: blue or gold or silver
Swimming would be just like mapping genealogy
Suggested boughs and branches with tendrils deep underwater

Notes

"When the otter drowned at Binder Park Zoo,": Binder Park Zoo, a zoo in Battle Creek, Michigan, is real. Mr. Sam, the dead otter, is not.

"Stain": Poem inspired by "Cut" by Sylvia Plath.

"Dear Ex-boyfriend,": Steve, I hope that wherever you are, you're happy. I know I am.

"The Sanderson Sisters Take Flight": These are characters from the 1993 movie *Hocus Pocus*, the best worst Halloween movie and one that was highly influential on my childhood.

"Pastoral #6": Lines in italics taken from *Wikipedia* page on Venetian blinds.

"The Ostriches Bathe in Tulsa, Oklahoma": The ostrich is, by far, the loveliest and most dangerous bird I have ever met. So much of love is danger. We are bound in a lovely, dangerous, rapturous love.

"Family Histories": Have you ever wondered why there are so many angels in the ocean?

Acknowledgments

The following poems or variations thereof have been published in these journals:

"A Trans Man's Guide to Using the Public Bathroom," *Volney Road Review* (2019)
"At the Stillwater, Oklahoma, Botanic Gardens," *The Ocotillo Review* (2020)
"Cosmetology," *Prospectus* (2021)
"Dressing as a Trans Man in the Early Morning," *Pittsburgh Poetry Review* (2018)
"Eulogy," *Coffin Bell Journal* (2021)
"Fire Eater, Premolar, Bone," *The Hunger* (2021)
"Fratercula Cirrhata, or Boy Crossing," *LandLocked* (2020)
"Ghazal for a Business Trip," *Sleet Magazine* (2019)
"Ghazal for the End of the World," *Grand Little Things* (2020)
"Head Space," Academy of American Poets (2019)
"Pastoral #1" and "Pastoral #6," *The Account* (2020)
"Prosopagnosia Feels Like Looking Through a Tunnel and Landing in a Graveyard," *Harpur Palate* (2021)
"Self-portrait as Ghost," *Rust + Moth* (2020)
"Sleep Paralysis," *Book of Matches* (2020)
"Sunrise," *Construction Literary Magazine* (2019)
"The Ostriches Bathe in Tulsa, Oklahoma," Academy of American Poets (2021)
"Vital Signs," *petrichor* (2021)
"Waking Up from Top Surgery in a Sparse Airbnb Living Room," *Rogue Agent* (2018)
"Walking with My Lover to Bury Our Dead Fish," *Frontier Poetry* (2021)
"When My Wife Cuts Her Hair & I Forget What to Say" and "Paris, Spring 2020," *Juked* (2021)
"When we don't invite your older brother to the wedding & your mother wants to know why," *Jet Fuel Review* (2020)

My life as a poet is indebted to many educators and mentors. Thank you, Mr. Sang, for teaching me how to sing; thank you, Dustin, for teaching me how to light fires; thank you, Nancy, Richard, & Steve, for your formative undergraduate workshops; thank you, Kim, for welcoming me to the WMU Writing Center family; thank you, Larissa, F. Dan, Sharona, Abby, & Becca, for a magical MFA experience; thank you, Janine, Lisa, Sarah Beth, & Dinah, for your invaluable mentorship at Oklahoma State University; thank you, Mrs. Shugars, for getting me through more than just math. The biggest thanks of all to my parents and sister for teaching me how to adventure.

Remi Recchia is a trans poet and essayist from Kalamazoo, Michigan. He is a Ph.D. student in English-Creative Writing at Oklahoma State University. He currently serves as an associate editor for the *Cimarron Review*. A three-time Pushcart Prize nominee, Remi's work has appeared in *Columbia Online Journal, Harpur Palate,* and *Juked,* among others. He holds an MFA in poetry from Bowling Green State University.

www.ingramcontent.com/pod-product-compliance
Lightning Source LLC
Chambersburg PA
CBHW030351100526
44592CB00010B/920